We Fell In "almosts"

A collection of what never was

Ritika Piplode

BookLeaf
Publishing

India | USA | UK

Made with ❤ on the BookLeaf Publishing Platform
www.bookleafpub.in
www.bookleafpub.com

Dedication

For the ones who remembers the almosts and the maybes.
For the hearts that stayed open even when love didn't return.

Preface

Love lingers in moments we almost had. This book is about the second kind- the kind that never found home , yet stayed anyway.

"We Fell in Almosts" is a collection of poems written from the feelings that never found words and stories that only lived in our hearts. The only thing we have is memories . The doors which we never locked but for which we lost the key .

Each poem is a piece of that journey - from the first glance of love - to deep connection - to heartbreak - to reflection - to quiet healing. Some of these poems were written in love, some in longing and some in the hope of letting go.

If you've ever loved someone who was never yours, If you've ever lived in the "almost" of a feeling — I hope you find yourself somewhere in these pages.

Acknowledgements

I would like to begin by thanking my elder brother and sister for guiding me through the process of writing this book, offering support at every step.

To my parents, thankyou for believing in me, encouraging my passion, and standing by me throughout this poetic journey .

To my close friends, who never doubted that one day I would write a book and call myself a poet— thank you for your faith, your cheer and for always reminding me to keep going.

Every word in this book carries a piece of your love, encouragement and belief, and for that I'm truly grateful.

The "date" it all began

It was 21st of December, when i first saw you
My eyes didn't meet yours, but my heart whispered it
was true.
You didn't notice me then, But I chose to wait,
Now you're looking at me, and it feels like fate.

Two years passed and seven days quietly flew,
Maybe winters are special for us, like skies turning blue.
Like the cold days and long nights, you came into my life
And now everything feels warmer, like sunshine after
ice.

On the eighth day, he spoke his heart out,
"You're the one I want, cant live without".
From the first glimpse to this moment, we've found
A love like rivers joining, endless and unbound.

When he fills my eyes

When I see him , the world stands still,
My heart surrenders to his will.
The chaos fade, the storm subside,
In his embrace, all fears I hide.

When I see him, the moonlight glows,
Soft as the love my spirit knows.
No whispered word, no need for sound,
His presence wraps me all around.

When I see him, time bends and sways,
A fleeting dream that never stays.
I reach for him— like clouds for rain,
Yet every touch sparks sweet pain.

I do not know what draw me near,
A silent pull so strong , so clear.
If only fate would grant me grace,
To love him long, to hold his space.

The "one " i see

When his eyes met mine,
I'm lost within their endless shine.
Everything turned black and white,
like stars that wake the silent night.

Wishing to play with his hairs,
while it blows in the air.
And attach all the flowers I love,
it dances like wings of a dove.

Every time my heart skips a beat when he smiles,his
smile shines bright, lighting up the skies.
It calms me down in a gentle way,
like finding peace at the end of the day.

I hold his hand for the first time,
like winter's cold breeze — so pure, so fine.
His hands look perfect resting in mine,
in his touch, I feel love's sign.

His voice is soft, like the sunrise,
hearing him is my favourite choice.
He doesn't speak much, but his eyes don't lie,
in every glance, they whisper why.

His heart is like my favourite flower — rose,
soft and gentle, where love still grows.
In the garden, it's the only flower I see,
I wish his heart could someday choose me.

I fell in love, twice!

For so long, I longed to confess,
but love reached late, beneath the skies.
My words fail me, my voice turns weak,
yet I hope you read it all in my eyes.

They say everything changes in love,
perhaps that's why I'm in love twice.
When you are near , even stars align,
and fireflies whisper ,"you are mine".

Your glimpse can brighten up my day,
words can't express this feeling inside.
No poet's verse could ever replace,
the way my heart falls twice, and thrice.

You're the one I hold above all ties,
my every prayer echoes my sighs.
I've told my love in countless cries—
now only my pillow knows why.

Whenever you're near, the world feels right,
my heart learns love in softer light.
I never knew what forever could do,
until I fell twice— in love with you.

Chosen pairs

I'm the day,
You're the date.
I'm the night,
You're the dream.

I'm the camera,
You're the photograph.
I'm the earplugs,
You're the song.

I'm the tree,
You're the leaf.
I'm the thorns,
You're the flower.

I'm the question,
You're the answer.
I'm the door,
You're the key.

I'm the book,
You're the chapter.
I'm an empty page,
You're the words.

I'm the touch,
You're the feeling.
I'm the scar,
You're the healing.

I'm the poet,
You're the muse.
I'm the canvas,
You're the hues.

I'm the month,
You're the season.
This is my writing,
and you're the reason.

Who's as pretty as the song...

So there's this guy,
Maybe it was his smile,
Or maybe it was his voice.
Maybe it was his kindness,
Or maybe it was his heart.

She don't know what it is,
But she fell pretty hard,
Fell pretty hard for the one...

Who's as pretty as the song that feels like the first word
of a love poetry,
The words I write keep alive his story.
Each line I write begins and ends with you,
My ink learns love in every shade and hue.

Who's as pretty as the song that feels like painting left
unfinished,
Every color bends to the shape of him.

The brush moves softly in my heart,
In this canvas of us, he's the masterpiece from the start.

Who's as pretty as the song that feels like home,
A place where I wish forever to roam.
Every room echoes the name of you more than me,
Home isn't a place, it's wherever you'll be.

Parallel hearts

Two hearts, two lines, never to meet,
Running together, yet incomplete.
She raced toward love, chasing the glow,
He walked beside her, steady and slow.

She spoke in whispers, he heard but stayed still,
She longed for fire, he craved for chill.
She reached for tomorrow, he lived in the past,
Two beating hearts— never meant to last.

She loved him from distance and watched from afar,
Her love was a book , his heart, never a scar.
He never saw the pages of her love.
A story she wrote , but he never read enough.

No heart could hold him the way hers does,
Like clock hands at 11:11 , frozen because.
Her love drew near , yet never reached him,
A circle of time, fading and dim.

One last time

One last time,
I want to see him near.
One last time,
To hold him close, sincere.

One last time ,
To watch him, heart unchained.
One last time,
To touch his hand, unstrained.

One last time,
To hug him, safe and tight.
One last time,
To feel his warmth, my light.

One last time,
To live a love so true.
One last time,
To know the world through you.

One last time ,
To believe he's mine, if only for a day.
One last time,
To whisper goodbye with love, not pain.

Can we just disappear?

Can we just disappear where buildings bends and sway,
And streets dissolve like smoke at the edge of day?
Just disappear where the city forgets to stay,
And we lose ourselves, then find our way.

We'll float in a dream we cannot own,
Where corridors and corners have paths we've never
known.
The breeze tastes of moments we've never flown,
And nothing obeys the rules we were shown.

Can we just disappear where walls taste of rain,
And windows hum secrets we cannot explain.
No footsteps to follow, no maps to fear,
Just us, nowhere and here.

After the fall

After the fall, you lose them, and it feels like heartbreak,
though they were never yours, no matter the chances
you'd take.
You searched for meaning in the quiet, aching space,
but sometimes silence is the truth you have to face.

It was something vast, too deep to define,
letting go cuts hard, but the pain softens with time. You
don't know how to close a door that never fully opened,
but time will teach you not to walk back to what's
broken.

The heart still aches, yet it's learning to mend,
in every tear, a strength begins to ascend.
Like a storm that fades, leaving the sky crystal clear,
the calm will arrive, and peace will draw near.

Hating myself, Loving you

I hate myself for the way I cared,
for every quiet prayer that you'd be there.
For how your name felt like a sheltered place,
and for I clung to you, refusing to erase.

I hate myself for craving your touch,
for trusting too blindly, for feeling too much.
For every tear that fell because of you,
for believing in dreams that were never true.

I hate myself for the way I smiled,
whenever your presence stays for a while.
For how my heart still forgets to beat,
each time your shadow and mine almost meet.

I hate myself for calling you my "first",
for thinking you'd heal what only got worse.
For building a home I wasn't meant to,
for loving someone who never knew.

I hate that I still search for your face,
In crowded rooms and empty space.
That no matter how much I try to undo,
some part of me still belongs to you.

I curse my heart that bled so true,
yet nothing has ever loved you more than I do.

The "*almost*" I buried

I'm in love, yet no one sees,
a trembling ache that crushes me.
I'm in love, yet none believe,
a heart can bleed and still breathe.

I'm in love, but he won't know,
that every thought is chained in woe.
I'm in love, yet he won't see,
how every breath is bound to thee.

My love is a secret, locked in pain,
ink bleeds the grief I cannot explain.
These pages hold my silent screams,
the love I live, the love that bleeds.

Each letter whispers what I hide,
each rose I saved guards my pride.
Each little thing, both old and new,
remembers a heart that only knew you.

Everyone who knows me, knows you too,
for in my eyes, your shadow breaks through.
So clear to me, yet hidden from sight.
A love that lingers, yet dies in quiet night.

Unsaid goodbye

I deserved a better goodbye,
both of us acting like strangers,
and we didn't even know how to say hi !

I deserved a better goodbye,
memories of us are still breathing,
because it was just you and I.

I deserved a better goodbye,
I loved you but couldn't say it,
for fear I'd lose you, and couldn't bear the cry.

I deserved a better goodbye,
things were left unsaid, and we drifted apart,
now you're gone and I'm left to wonder why.

It's the month of July,
my messages were waiting for your reply,
but you never spoken again and gave me
A forever goodbye.

The meeting that never came

And we never met again,
tears slipped quietly in the night,
Memories of us replayed in the dark,
yet you never knew my world lost light.

And we never met again,
I swore I wouldn't whisper your name,
Yet longing rose with every storm,
and every tear still felt the same.

And we never met again,
you walked away; I watched you go,
To you, love was just a fleeting flame,
to me, a wound that healed too slow.

And we never met again,
the world moved on, but I stood still,
Listening for echoes in empty air,
Searching for signs only memory could spill.

With you, without you, I lost my way,
chasing dreams that bled in vain.
Yet one question haunts my soul—
Why did we never meet again?

Echoes of what she gave

She craves love but didn't get though,
Her heart was a garden where no flower grows.
She waits for a touch that never came,
They turned the pages, but never learned her name.

Her soul writes letters no eyes have read,
like roses she placed on graves of the dead.
She gives her all, but ends in pain,
her tears dissolve in the pouring rain.

She still waters the roots that never grew,
Hoping someone they'll bloom too.
Planting her heart into barren ground,
As petals fall, the only cries without a sound.

She gathers the echoes of what she gave,
Lingers among memories she cannot save.
She craves love but didn't get though,
Her heart was a garden where no flower grows.

A poem no one heard

I felt bad when my words were left unread,
like letters gathering dust on a forgotten shelf.
Each syllable drifted away with the wind,
A story abandoned, losing itself.

I felt bad when my words couldn't speak,
the depth of my soul, the ache it keeps.
Like a song without melody, lost in the hush,
Or a poem that quietly weeps.

I felt bad when my words never reached,
like a bird that falls before it learned to fly.
No echoes returned, just silence remained,
A tale, unfinished, ignored with a sigh.

Maybe my words never mattered at all,
like a candle unlit in the loneliest night.
And I stood there holding the match in my hand,
But they never longed for light.

Did my poetry fade like footprints in sand ?
It hurts when no one is there to understand.

I am in love with the impossibility of us

I am in love with snow that never melts,
Chilling my hands, yet warming my heart.
We dance in frost, yet never meet,
Love drifts away on winter's sheet.

I am in love with wires that can never be tangled,
The shape of us— impossible, forever angled.
Electric threads where fingers can't trace,
A hidden current no hand can chase.

I am in love with leaves that drinks the sun, yet never
dries,
A silent hope that never denies.
It breathes in sun, we cannot claim,
Fragile heart having no name.

I am in love with safety pins that aren't safe,
Tears telling the love we crave.

Hearts balancing by delicate trust,
I am in love with the impossibility of us.

Lost poems, Found by Rain

My poetry packed its bag and left his door,
It found a place where raindrops pour.
They kiss the rain instead of his skin,
Trusting the clouds more than I trusted him.

Thunder reads every line I wrote in the night,
It gathers my verses too far from his sight.
I wonder where my poems now lay,
Washing the ache of him quietly away.

Letters I sent to the rain now lie somewhere lost,
Droplets carry my heart where he never crossed.
Poems that spoke of him now dance with the breeze,
Finding their home among rivers and trees.

The muse has left, still my ink flows upon the page,
The rain now listens, calming every rage.
The storm carries the fragments of who I was,
Mending the spaces where my heart once paused.

Paper moons and Empty hands

Paper moons float across my windowpane,
I trace your absence with fingers grown faint.
Casting fragile light against the darkened skies,
And map the quiet shape where my sorrow lies.

Empty hands hold nothing but air,
Memories settle like dust everywhere.
The echo of laughter that lingered too long,
I hum them softly like my favourite song.

Drawings of us curl on paper thin ,
Edges torn by the weight of what has been.
I fold them gently, letting the past rest,
Finding small peace within my chest.

Glass jars hold our once- burning flame,
Tiny fragments of us, now no longer the same.

I watch them shimmer in the fading quiet night,
Learning that letting go can feel "almost" right.

Sat by window, made the little paper moons,
With empty hands , sensing their fragile tunes.
I place each wish upon a star, tucked safely in a glass jar,
I let it go , healing slowly from every scar.

Fragments in Ink

Muse, for whom poets sailed in inked seas,
Their hearts spilled verses on quiet breeze.
Each line had flickered like a dying flame,
Marking the shape of a love that once had came.

Art, for whom artists lose their way,
In woods of thoughts where shadows play.
My art wanders where my soul once roamed,
Now whispers softly, " you're still at home".

Nostalgia, danced in the folds of my mind,
I traced the echoes of the love we left behind.
Each moment had whispered secrets of the past,
Shaping the fragments that could not last.

Affection lingered in quiet corners, yearning grew,
I wrote for the one who never knew.
Still joy remains from what I gave,
The love I kept, the heart I saved.

Healing had opened the heart once closed,
I breathed the truths I once had supposed.
Each fear had dissolved like dew on autumn leaves,
Settling soft hues where the heart once grieves.

Kissed my art in my poems once more,
I painted with hues on the skin we'd known.
Goodbyes are like spilled coffee on old pages,
Leaving the stains of my love through ages.

I wish the imprints of my poems stay on your mind,
When you see your name in my rhymes.
Join each initial and create a new word,
I hope you find what I love.

We fell in love"almosts"

I've read somewhere,
Today is the first day, I saw 11:11
and didn't think of you.
But we fell in "almosts ",

Sometimes when I first saw you on the ground,
Or when our paths crossed on the staircase.
I felt my chest tighten without a sound,
like glass cracking slowly in empty space.

Sometimes when I looked for you through a window,
Or sat an under a tree just to watch you from far.
Your laughter spilled softly, golden and yellow,
and I trace it like a secret scar.

Sometimes when I handed you the bracelet you never
wore ,
Or pressed a rose between the pages of my diary.
Each bead fell like raindrops on the floor,
And I kept it close, as my forever favourite memory.

33

I kept my "almosts" played like lanterns lost at sea,
Each one heartbeat I couldn't let fall,
Even when nothing else felt certain to me,
I love every fragment, every quiet call.

Though we never touched the sky or sank to the floor,
Every stolen moment of all we had lost,
And in the quiet of memory, I find my core,
And in the maybes, our souls danced, but-
We fell in "almosts."

www.ingramcontent.com/pod-product-compliance
Lightning Source LLC
Chambersburg PA
CBHW050954030426
42339CB00007B/386